Curls Are My Confidence!

Shai Nesbit and Jaxon Brown

Spirit Filled Creations

Curls Are My Confidence
Copyright © 2023 Jaxon Brown and Shai Nesbit
www.curlsaremyconfidence.com

Published by Spirit Filled Creations LLC
www.SpiritFilledCreations.com
Email: SpiritFilledCreations7@gmail.com

This book or parts thereof may not be reproduced in any form, stored in a retrieval system, or transmitted in any form by any means – electronic, mechanical, photocopy, recording, or otherwise – without prior written permission of the publisher and authors, except as provided by United States of America copyright law.

All rights reserved.

International Standard Book Number: 978-1-7342948-8-0

First Edition, Hardcover

Printed in the United States of America

This book is dedicated to all kids who will confidently take on this world with their smiles and curls, to all kids who will influence society and feel confident to express their beautiful blackness in all their natural hair stages. We hope that kids worldwide will stumble upon this book with a special moment of discovery and secret power, knowing that there's no one quite like them!

A special thank you to our beautiful mommies who helped us write this book! We have the best mommies ever!

Let's change the world one curl and one smile at a time. With our curls, we will travel the world.

Curl one, curl two, and curl three.

I'm Jaxon.

Curls in all colors, shapes, and sizes, just like you and me. We are two special kids...

...and I'm Shai.

From the beginning, we were two special gifts,

With the best curls ever, waiting to give the world a lift.

The day we were born, there were no clouds in the skies... here comes Jaxon with sandy, brown hair and Shai with her bright, glassy brown eyes.

We are black, bold, and have big hair, but who we are doesn't stop there.

We are beautiful, strong, handsome, and smart.

Some people say our hair is a piece of art.

It's okay
if everyone
does not
understand
our crown,

it's ours to own,
so we won't frown!

We are always showing love and like to be fair, on our journey meeting new people around town as we dare.

Not only would we become the best of friends but the world would be ours to conquer and on long summer days we would spend.

Did you know your curls had power?

Silly girl, no way! How? You mean like the Eiffel Tower.

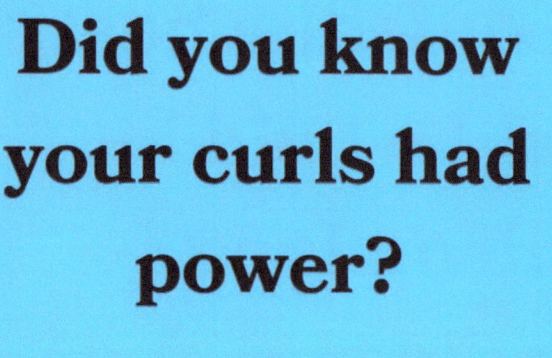

Yes, each strand, with strength and uniqueness we can change the world, with our hair and hand.

Our curls are waiting to explode, just like the friendship we now hold.

Soft, curly, coily and tight, but never too much and always just right.

Long, luscious, wild, and free, that's what our curls mean to me!

If our hair looks different than yours, it's okay,

God gave us all something different our heart endures.

We'll always have special hair and a friendship from the start, but what sets us apart is our kind and loving heart.

Be confident in all that you do!
Remember, it's what's inside,
that's what makes you, You!

Like kindness, creativity and thoughtful things you do! Know that God has put something special in you.

Spread kindness, joy, and love to everyone.
Seeing each other smile is so much fun!

And when those curls grow bigger than your hand, remember God created them strand by strand.

And if those curls feel like too much to tame, remember God created you in His special name.

Well, until the next time we meet in an aquarium looking at a shark, or on the playground at the park, just look for us, two curly-head best friends, Jaxon and Shai.
The end.

Curls are my Confidence is a heartwarming and empowering children's book written by young talents Jaxon Brown and Shai Nesbit. This beautifully illustrated tale follows the journey of two friends, embracing their unique curly hair and discovering the strength and confidence that lies within. As the duo navigates various adventures and life lessons, they inspire the importance of being fair and kind, and they learn the importance of self-love, individuality, and celebrating the differences that make them who they are.

Aimed at children aged 4-8, Curls Are My Confidence encourages young readers to embrace their natural beauty or masculinity and fosters an early understanding of self-acceptance, inclusivity, and kindness. This charming and inspiring story is a must-read for parents and educators seeking to foster a positive self-image and instill the values of diversity and self-love in the hearts of the next generation.

Shai Bailey Nesbit is a vivacious, spunky five-year-old who never meets a stranger! Shai is known for her big curly hair and her big heart to match. She is a lover of all things glam, especially Barbie. Shai enjoys dancing, playing with friends, school, and making memories with her little sister and big brother. Shai is sure to leave you with a smile on your face!

You can follow @_theshaishow_ on Instagram and The Shai Show on YouTube to keep up with Shai.

Thank you for supporting our new book with your orders and helping us instill confidence one curl at a time!

Jaxon Emory Brown is a talented, smart, and caring five-year-old who loves to dance! His sandy brown hair and coily fro can be spotted a mile away! Jaxon loves playing with friends, jumping off anything above him lol, sharing hugs and kisses with his baby sister, and any athletic activity with his older brother! He has BIG HAIR but a BIGGER HEART, and he's sure to make you laugh with his dance moves! 🕺📚

You can follow Jaxon @curlsaremyconfidence on Instagram.

Thank you for supporting our new book with your orders and helping us instill confidence one curl at a time!

Printed in the USA
CPSIA information can be obtained
at www.ICGtesting.com
LVHW071642031023
759759LV00088B/215